More FAITH

L.I.F.E. Apps-Devotions
Living in Faith Every Day

Life applications are short devotions
to strengthen, equip, and encourage Christians
to live in faith every day.

Tammy Dozier Trusty

More Faith. L.I.F.E. Apps-Devotions for Living in Faith Every Day Book 2

Edited by Terah Trusty
Cover Art by Tina Swinford

ISBN 987-1-7333351-3-3
Published by: From the Heart Books LLC. United States

Amplified Bible, The Lockman Foundation, 1999-2015.
The Living Bible, Tyndale House Publishers, Inc, 1971.
New International Version, Biblica, 2011-2016.
NIV Once-A-Day Bible for Women, Zondervan, 2012.
The Message, NavPress Publishing Group, 2002.
New Living Translation, 1996, 2004, 2015 by Tyndale House Foundation.
Amplified Bible, Classic Edition, 1954, 1958, 1962, 1964, 1965, 1987 by The Lockman Foundation.

All praise and thanks to my Savior, Jesus Christ!

Dedicated to my wonderful parents. Thank you for all the love and support through the years! I thank God for you!!I love you!

Other books written by the author:
L.I.F.E. Apps-Devotions for Living in Faith Every Day! (Book 1)
L.I.F.E. Apps Journal (Book 1)
Find them on Amazon.

.

www.tammytrusty.com

www.facebook.com/tammydoziertrustyauthor

Letter to the reader,

I have always written better than I talk. When I was younger, I was shy. I did not speak well and rarely if there were strangers or adults near that I did not know. As I grew, I lacked the confidence to even talk to others and definitely did not speak up unless I was around close friends and family.

Through the years, I have put words on paper to express myself whether it is writing a devotion, a note to encourage a friend, stories, poems, studying scripture, writing prayers, or journaling my feelings or prayers

What I lack is what God will use! Where I lack confidence, He infuses His confidence. It just proves that He is God. By His Spirit, His power, His strength, and His grace I can do anything that He calls me to do! I hope you enjoy the devotions and that they encourage you, motivate you, and bring you revelation from the Word of God. I pray that you are encouraged to live by faith every day and have More Faith after reading this book.

Blessings,

Tammy Dozier Trusty

Used by God

How does God want to use you? You should trust that He will give you all you need for what He calls you to do. God does not pick the qualified; instead, He qualifies the called! There's a divine download waiting for you, just ask!! Now step out of the boat!

Now to Him who is able to [carry out His purpose and] do superabundantly more than all that we dare ask or think [infinitely beyond our greatest prayers, hopes, or dreams], according to His power that is at work within us.

(*The Amplified Bible*, Ephesians 3:20)

Looking Forward

I look forward to the new year with hope and expectation. I ask God for a word for the year. Sometimes it's a word or phrase like balance, trust me, or just do it. Sometimes it's a verse to stand on like Proverbs 3:5-6. I always write it down in my prayer journal and on a notecard and put it on my mirror. It's just a reminder of what I should focus on throughout the year.

May you get a word, phrase, or verse to stand on this year that will encourage you. My word this year is Go Forward with God! He is wanting me to step out of the boat! Go forward with God! Have faith that the new year brings you lots of great possibilities!

Brethren, I count not myself to have apprehended:
but this one thing I do,
forgetting those things which are behind, and reaching forth unto those things which are before,
I press toward the mark for the prize
of the high calling of God in Christ Jesus.

(*King James Version*, Philippians 3:12-14)

Faith in Jesus

Today is your day! If you have been reading all about Jesus and haven't ever invited Him to come into your life or heart, today is your day! What better way to start the year than to give your life to God. Reading about Him and talking about Him doesn't mean that you know Him.

Today is the day, and this is the year to get to know God better. The door to God is open by coming through his Son, Jesus. Jesus is the way to God.

Invite Jesus into your life. He will be your Savior and Lord. He will be a constant source of comfort. He will be your faithful companion. He will be your way to know God.

We all need a Savior! Today is your day!

If you declare with your mouth, "Jesus is Lord," and believe in your heart that God raised him from the dead, you will be saved. For it is with your heart that you believe and are justified, and it is with your mouth that you profess your faith and are saved.
(*New International Version,* Romans 10:9-10)

God Goals

I do not make resolutions anymore. For years I made resolutions, and I always failed. A new diet lasted about two weeks. A resolution never lasted very long, then I would feel condemnation. It's not good to start the year off with failure so I had to make changes.

Now I try to reflect on the past year and look forward to the new one. I try to make God goals. I write down my goals. It isn't something I have to do every day. It's something I would like to finish sometime this year. I commit my life to God and ask Him to give me the wisdom, grace, motivation, and favor that I need to get it done. A God goal is less pressure, and I am more confident that I can accomplish it with God's help.

When I picture a target, it has circles all around the center. I can hit all around it. I think it's pretty good, but with God and faith, I can hit the bull's eye! That's a God goal. What are your goals for this year?

> I can do all things through Christ which strengtheneth me.
>
> (*King James Version*, Philippians 4:13)

4

God is Faithful!

His love!
His mercy!
His forgiveness!
His grace!
His peace!
His healing!
His comfort!
His provision!
His wisdom!
His guidance!
His strength!
His power!
His salvation!
His promises!
His presence!
His Spirit!
His Son!
His Word!
His blessings!

God is faithful, by whom ye were called
unto the fellowship of his Son Jesus Christ
our Lord.

(*King James Version*, 1 Corinthians 1:9)

Faith

It takes faith to stand when you cannot see the victory yet. Faith will move mountains. Don't let logic and reasoning push away faith. Stand on the Word. Stand on the promises of God. Put your trust in Him! Stand in faith!!

> What is faith? It is the confident assurance that something we want is going to happen. It is the certainty that what we hope for is waiting for us, even though we cannot see it up ahead. Men of God in days of old were famous for their faith.
>
> (*The Living Bible*, Hebrews 11:1-2)

The Cross

When I think about the cross I am so thankful for God's love and Jesus' sacrifice! How could someone take our punishment and our sin? Each wound, the pain, betrayal, and each step of the way to the cross was for us. Each moment on the cross was for us. The whole purpose of Jesus coming to earth was for us. I don't fully comprehend it, but I am tremendously grateful for God's mercy, grace, love, and salvation. Thank you, God, for the cross! Help me understand it even more!

It is of the Lord's mercies that we are not consumed, because his compassions fail not. They are new every morning: great is thy faithfulness.

(*King James Version*, Lamentations 3:22-23)

Have Faith!

Stand strong and courageous! Stand upright, rooted and grounded in Christ Jesus. Go forward in victory and strength. You are the light of the world, the salt of the earth, and ambassadors for Christ. You are more than conquerors through Christ Jesus. You can do all things through Christ which strengthens you. You are an overcomer. Greater is He that is in you than he that is in the world. You are making a difference!

Oh, mighty child of God, you are victorious through Christ Jesus!

> But thanks be to God, which giveth us the victory through our Lord Jesus Christ.
>
> (*King James Version*, 1 Corinthians 5:15)

Trust God

Once my husband and I found ourselves driving up a huge bridge. We couldn't see beyond the highest point. It went up so far that it seemed to disappear. The road could have just stopped without us realizing it. We could have just fell into the water below. We didn't know what was ahead but had to trust that the road extended beyond the top point.

It was scary to me. I don't like heights, and the unknown can be scary. I knew that the road had to go on. We drove on slowly while other cars familiar with that bridge drove quickly passing us. Of course, there was a road, and we drove safely to the other side.

Life can be like that. The unknown path can be scary. Change is scary, but God will lead us safely to the other side. Rest assured, He is with you! Don't be afraid! Have faith! Take courage! Trust God!

Trust in the Lord with all thine heart; and lean not unto thine own understanding. In all thy ways acknowledge him, and he shall direct thy paths.

(*New International Version*, Proverbs 3:5-6)

The Center

The book of Nehemiah has so many truths that are helpful to me. I love studying it! Nehemiah was the king's cupbearer. He was near the king. He had favor with the king. He was willing to lay down his life for the king. Because he was close to the king, he was given favor to go rebuild the walls of Jerusalem.

It reminded me that like Nehemiah we should be close to our King. He should be the center of our life and seated on the throne of our hearts. He is our fortress, our hiding place, our Rock, our high tower. When we are in the center of His will we have His favor. We are strong. We are safe! We are victorious!

Let God be the center of your life, thoughts, decisions, words, and actions. Let Him take center stage in your life.

He that dwelleth in the secret place of the most High shall abide under the shadow of the Almighty. I will say of the Lord, He is my refuge and my fortress: my God; in him will I trust.

(*King James Version*, Psalm 91:1-2)

Don't Give Up

It was the bottom of the sixth. The score was tied. All night the opposing team had scored run after run. Then we would come up to bat and have to catch up. All the fans were clapping and yelling. Now we had to play one more inning to break the tie. The other team batted first. They scored run after run. It looked like there was no stopping them. They were just five years old. Some of them were playing in the dirt or distracted so they didn't even see the ball go past them. Several raced after a hit ball and fought over it letting the other team score five runs! Finally, we got three outs.

Now we could win it with six runs or lose. The odds were not in our favor. That is a lot of runs. This was it. We could win or lose the championship right here. I don't think the boys even realized how close they were to winning.

They didn't give up though. They didn't say we can't get six runs. They didn't say we can't do it. In fact, they played their hardest and came from behind to score six runs to win the championship for their Little League Division. It didn't look like they could do it, but they did because they didn't quit!

It may not look good right now to you. It may not look like you're going to beat this. It may not look like you're going to get through it, but with God, things can change quickly. You can do this. Victory is yours. God is on your side!

Don't give up. Don't give in. Don't throw in the towel. You can still come from behind and be a winner. Have faith in God!

> I can do all things through Christ which strengtheneth me.
>
> (*King James Version*, Philippians 4:13)

Good Thoughts

Some days we get a lot of mail, so we have to sort through it. I throw out all the junk mail. Some days I get more junk mail than others. Just like our mail, we get a lot of thoughts that are junk. If your thoughts are negative or don't line up with the Word of God, then they should be thrown in the trash. Thoughts of condemnation, jealousy, rejection, or unforgiveness are junk. Junk mail comes in the form of put-downs, distractions, stress, fear, doubt, and worry. Any thoughts that God wouldn't agree with are junk mail. Get rid of them quickly!

Our thoughts can really affect our day. We need to think good thoughts. We need to think about the Word of God. We need to have our thoughts filled with faith. Encouraging thoughts inspire us and bring us peace of mind. What are you thinking?

Finally, brethren, whatsoever things are true, whatsoever things are honest, whatsoever things are just, whatsoever things are pure, whatsoever things are lovely, whatsoever things are of good report; if there be any virtue, and if there be any praise, think on these things.

(*King James Version*, Philippians 4:8)

Give it to God!

Talking about a problem helps because it gets things off your chest, but when we give it to God through prayer, it is even better. Prayer acknowledges that we can't do anything about it, but God can. Giving it to God is better than just thinking and worrying about it. That does absolutely nothing to help. There is nothing that we can do about a situation except give it to God. Have faith in God. Let go. Let God!

Don't hold on to your problems, give them to God!!

> But you are to hold fast to the Lord your God, as you have until now.
>
> (*New International Version*, Joshua 23:8)

Follow the Leader

"Follow His leading with every part of your being." Adam Ward

Did you ever dance on your daddy's feet when you were little? I loved his complete attention. He led me around. I went wherever he went. It was better than playing follow the leader because I was safe and secure on him. He wouldn't let me fall off. He wouldn't let go. He was leading, and I was going with him every step of the way.

I want my life to be like that. I want to stand on my Father's feet and go everywhere that He goes. I know that He won't let go. I know that I can trust Him. Where He leads, I will follow!

> And the Lord, he it is that doth go before thee; he will be with thee, he will not fail thee, neither forsake thee: fear not, neither be dismayed.
>
> (*King James Version*, Deuteronomy 31:8)

God's Calling

God doesn't see who we are but who we can become. He sees our potential. He sees our possibilities. He sees our future.

He didn't just see a young shepherd boy when he looked at David. He saw a giant killer and a future King. He saw a man after his own heart.

He didn't see Peter as a fisherman or a coward that denied him three times. He saw him as a fisher of men and a future evangelist that would lead thousands to Christ.

He didn't see a young orphan girl when he saw Esther. He saw a future bride of the king that would save a whole nation because she was at the right place at the right time.

He didn't see Saul the Christian persecutor. He saw Paul a dynamic witness for Jesus that would write many books of the New Testament.

He doesn't see you how you see yourself. He sees a great future. He knows that you will succeed. Remember He is still working on you. Rise up and be who God is calling you to be. Don't settle for less.

> And we know that in all things God works for the good of those who love him, who have been called according to his purpose. (*King James Version*, Romans 8:28)

Questions for God

God, I need you. Are you here?
I AM.

God, help me.
I AM.

God, heal me.
I AM.

God, give me peace.
I AM.

God, give me love.
I AM.

God, give me finances.
I AM.

God, give me wisdom.
I AM.

God, give me strength.
I AM.

God, give me Jesus.
I did!

> God said to Moses, "I am who I am. This is what you are to say to the Israelites: 'I am has sent me to you.'"
> (*New International Version*, Exodus 3:14)

Go!! Team Jesus!!!

Come on, Team. Let's gather around Coach Jesus. What does He have to say today?!

"You can do this! Together we've got this. I have your back. Follow My lead. Do as I say, and you will win this one. It might look tough, but I'll push you and help you along the way. Go out and represent Me. Be the light! Trust me! You have got this! Today is our victory!

Go, Team Jesus!!"

> Therefore, my dear brothers and sisters, stand firm. Let nothing move you. Always give yourselves fully to the work of the Lord, because you know that your labor in the Lord is not in vain.
>
> (*New International Version*, 1 Corinthians 15:58)

Don't Quit!

Sometimes I just want to quit! But, quitters never win, and winners never quit. Look at all the people that failed but never gave up: Abraham Lincoln, Thomas Edison, and Paul of Tarsus just to name a few. They didn't quit when the going got tough, but they kept trying. They worked hard. They were determined to stay the course. Winners never quit. They get back up when they fall down. They try again! They are persistent!

Get up! Get going! Keep going! Don't let failure or missteps hold you back! Stand tall, look forward, and keep going strong! You can do it!

> Brethren, I count not myself to have apprehended: but this one thing I do, forgetting those things which are behind, and reaching forth unto those things which are before, I press toward the mark for the prize of the high calling of God in Christ Jesus.
>
> (*King James Version*, Philippians 3:13-14)

Give

Notice this verse doesn't say when you give. It says give! Give! Be generous! Be helpful. Be kind. Give and give and give! Never stop! When you give, it has a boomerang effect. It will return to you pouring over you like a perpetual fountain. Waves of grace, mercy, peace, love, and favor will come in like the tide washing over you.

> Give, and it will be given to you. A good measure, pressed down, shaken together and running over, will be poured into your lap. For with the measure you use, it will be measured to you."
>
> (*New International Version*, Luke 6:38)

Challenges

Many of you are going through a difficult season. You are facing challenges that are stressful. Just a few years ago, I was having a very difficult time. I had been pushed to the brink of a meltdown. The stress and strain were unbelievable. One day driving down the road with tears streaming down my face, I cried out to God, "I can't do this anymore. It's just too hard."

God reassured me with these words, "It's only a season."

That set me free. I thought, "I can do a season. Seasons change. They don't last long." Do you know what happened? That season changed within a few months.

Now God says to you, "It's only for a season. You can handle this. I am right here with you. Don't give up now. You CAN do this. This season is about to change."

But I trust in you, Lord; I say, "You are my God." My times are in your hands; deliver me from the hands of my enemies, from those who pursue me. Let your face shine on your servant; save me in your unfailing love.

(*King James Version*, Psalms 31:14-16)

Got Jesus?

When you have Jesus, you can have:

Hope instead of hopelessness!
Love instead of hate!
Faith instead of fear!
Favor instead of rejection!
Strength instead of weakness!
Peace instead of worry!
Health instead of sickness!
Forgiveness instead of condemnation!
Wisdom instead of foolishness!
Rest instead of struggle!
Victory instead of defeat!

Now to Him who is able to [carry out His purpose and] do superabundantly more than all that we dare ask or think [infinitely beyond our greatest prayers, hopes, or dreams], according to His power that is at work within us, to Him be the glory in the church and in Christ Jesus throughout all generations forever and ever. Amen.

(*The Amplified Bible*, Ephesians 3:20-21)

A Work in Progress!

Cakes are not finished until all the ingredients are measured, mixed, baked, iced, and decorated. Then you have a finished product-a beautiful delicious dessert. But, it takes time!

It is the same way with us. We are like a cake that God is preparing. He is adding different ingredients to each of us like more patience, courage, faith, wisdom, maturity, truth, or helping us learn to trust Him more, to walk in love, compassion, and mercy. On the other hand, He may be adjusting the oven temperature burning out the pride, unbelief, fear, worry, and such. We will not be finished until God has prepared us just right! He is still working on us! The finished product is the very best YOU!

> Being confident of this very thing, that he which hath begun a good work in you will perform it until the day of Jesus Christ.
>
> (*New International Version*, Philippians 1:6)

Follow the Leader

I heard the children giggling and talking. I walked around the room as they follow behind me in a line. I put my arms up like I was flying. So, they did the same. I went around the desk. They followed me. I jumped up and down like a bunny. I heard them hopping. Then I crawled under the table. The giggles got louder as they each approached the table. I heard kids say, "Go under there. Follow her." Then the best one of all. I zigzagged through the back of the line. Playing follow the leader was always fun at VBS.

By following the leader and doing all that the leader does, you are doing well. It's just like following Jesus and doing his will. We have His Holy Spirit in us that leads us. The Bible is also our source of wisdom and direction. When we say that we have to follow Jesus, it means by knowing Him, His Word, and with the Holy Spirit's leading.

Let the Holy Spirit be your leader. Let Him guide you through every easy path and rocky road. Ask Him to teach you to understand His Word

> But the Comforter, which is the Holy Ghost, whom the Father will send in my name, he shall teach you all things, and bring all things to your remembrance, whatsoever I have said unto you.
> (*King James Version*, John 14:26)

Be Thankful

I woke up with these words on my mind, "He is good. He is good, and His love endures." David repeated that phrase in every verse in Psalm 136.

His heart was overflowing with thanksgiving because God's love endures. It goes on and on and on! It is never ending. Let's think about that today. Be thankful for His love!

> O give thanks unto the Lord; for he is good: for his mercy endureth for ever.
>
> (*King James Version*, Psalm 136:1)

Change

Change isn't fun. Who wants it? When we mention change, don't you just want to run the other way?! Let's look at change differently. Change can be good. It can shake us out of complacency and shake off the cobwebs that hinder us. It can bring life to a stagnant situation.

Something good can come from change. Think of it as a new door opening. An adventure! It's shaking off what holds you back. Look forward to new opportunities. It can bring new life! It can be invigorating and challenging! Will it be easy? Maybe or maybe not. Will it be scary? Maybe. Can you do it? Yes! God is with you!!

> Trust in the Lord with all thine heart; and lean not unto thine own understanding. In all thy ways acknowledge him, and he shall direct thy paths.
>
> (*King James Version*, Proverbs 3:5-6)

The Wait

Waiting can seem long, difficult, and hopeless. It can be a scary, dark time. It can be confusing, but take hope in the waiting. God has a plan. He is at work in your situation. You are not alone in the waiting. David was running and hiding from the king before he ever became king. Lazarus was brought back to life after four days in the tomb. Daniel was safe in the lion's den. Esther saved her people. Sarah conceived a child at an old age. Moses led the Israelites across on dry ground through the sea. Jesus was with the three Hebrew boys in the fiery furnace. Jesus arose on the third day. That which seemed hopeless was turned around. God received all the glory!

I can't wait to see what God is doing! I can't wait to hear more praise reports and testimonies about God's goodness. God is moving. The waiting is almost over! Be patient. Be hopeful. May God be glorified!

Why, my soul, are you downcast? Why so disturbed within me? Put your hope in God, for I will yet praise him, my Savior and my God.

(*New International Version*, Psalm 42:5)

Mighty Children of God!

Oh, mighty children of God!

You are victorious! You are overcomers!

You are trees planted by the living water
with your roots deep in the soil of God's Word.

You will not be shaken.

You will not be bend. You will not be uprooted.

You are strong in Lord and the power of His
might!

That person is like a tree planted by
streams of water, which yields its fruit in
season and whose leaf does not wither—
whatever they do prospers.

(*New International Version*, Psalms 1:3)

Who Does God Use?

Nehemiah was close to King Artaxerxes because he was his cupbearer. The king noticed his sadness and asked him what was wrong. He was sad that Jerusalem was destroyed and the gates were burned. He felt led to go rebuilt the city walls. He was given the okay by the king and sent with letters and an army of men. He set out to do the work of the Lord with God on his side and the king on his side. He was highly favored.

God chose him. He was the cupbearer, not a nobleman, not a king, and not a commander of a large army. God chose a simple man, a responsible man, a faithful man, an obedient man, a man of God, a man of faith. He chose Nehemiah for such a time as this not because he was important, rich, or able but because he was willing.

Commit your work to Him. God uses ordinary men and women to accomplish His work on earth. What is He calling you to do? Go do it! You have the favor of the Lord.

May the favor of the Lord our God rest on us; establish the work of our hands for us— yes, establish the work of our hands.

(*New International Version*, Psalm 90:17)

Don't Worry

One year when I was at church camp as a teacher, I was studying my lesson in an open-air chapel. The chapel had a good, sturdy roof over it, but three of the sides were open. I remember being worried and praying about the lesson that I was going to teach. I was studying my lesson for the day which was in Matthew 6 about the birds of the air and the lilies of the field.

All of a sudden, these little birds flew over my head into the chapel. They made their way to a little nest in the corner of the ceiling. It was a hidden nest. It was safe and secure from all the weather and wind. It was shady. It was much better being under a wooden roof than being in a tree. It reminded me that if God takes care of the sparrows then I don't have to worry because He is taking care of me, too.

So, if God takes care of the lilies of the field and the birds of the air, won't He take care of you, too?!

Look at the birds of the air; they do not sow or reap or store away in barns, and yet your heavenly Father feeds them. Are you not much more valuable than they? Can any one of you by worrying add a single hour to your life?

(*New International Version*, Matthew 6:26-27)

Mary and Martha

In Luke 10, Mary and Martha are sisters, but they are doing different things. Mary takes advantage of sitting at Jesus' feet. She gives him her full attention. She's doing what Jesus said is the best thing. She's getting to know him more. She's learning. She's listening. She's focused.

Mary is distracted. She has other things to do, so she gets caught up her work. She's busy working in the kitchen. Then she gets frustrated because Mary isn't helping her. If she would sit down with Jesus and take the time to be in his presence, she would have more peace. She wouldn't be so frustrated or upset.

This reminds me that I should give Jesus my full attention. I should take the time to sit in his presence, read the Word, study, and pray. Instead, I tend to be more like Martha, easily distracted by the things of the world. I tend to be too busy.

I want to sit at Jesus' feet listening to what He saying so that I am ready for the day. I want to listen, learn, and focus on Him. Sitting in His presence fills me with what I need-wisdom, guidance, energy, strength, encouragement, comfort, love, joy, faith, and peace.

Be like Mary! Get filled up!

And Jesus answered and said unto her, Martha, Martha, thou art careful and troubled about many things: But one thing is needful: and Mary hath chosen that good part, which shall not be taken away from her.

(*King James Version*, Luke 10:41-42)

Don't be Afraid

Even if the mountains fall into the sea, I shouldn't be afraid?! Really!

Even if everything around me is falling apart?

Even if the storm is overtaking me?

Even if I can't see anything besides the mountain in front of me, I should trust God? Yes!

Trust God! He can handle it. He has got this!

God is our refuge and strength, an ever-present help in trouble. Therefore we will not fear, though the earth give way and the mountains fall into the heart of the sea, though its waters roar and foam and the mountains quake with their surging.

(*King James Version*, Psalms 46:1-3)

Delight

Don't you take great pleasure when your child or grandchild says I love you! When they wrap those little arms around your neck and hug you tight, that is one of the sweetest things on earth! It just melts my heart!

Guess what? God delights in us, His children, when we tell Him we love Him. We should do it often. We should thank him, pray to him, praise Him, and love Him. God delights in our love for him.

His pleasure is not in the strength of the horse, nor his delight in the legs of the warrior; the Lord delights in those who fear him, who put their hope in His unfailing love.

(*New International Version*, Psalms 147:10-11)

God's Favor

Even with God's favor the enemy still attacked Nehemiah. Since he was doing what the Lord put on his heart to do, you would think it would be easy. It wasn't. He had opposition even when he was doing the Lord's work.

When God calls you to do something, don't back down when opposition comes your way! Recognize it as the enemy trying to get you off track.

Don't be stopped by the enemy. Don't get distracted. Press on! Push through the opposition! Stand your ground! Have faith in God! You have God's favor. He will grant you success!

Have not I commanded thee?
Be strong and of a good courage;
be not afraid,
neither be thou dismayed:
for the Lord thy God is with thee
whithersoever thou goest.

(*King James Version*, Joshua 1:9)

Jesus Loves Me!

When I was a child, I often sang the song, "Jesus loves me." One day at church when I was an adult the speaker said that we should sing it and really listen to the words. The entire congregation sang it acapella. All the voices created a beautiful sound! But better than the sound were the words that spoke to my heart.

Have you stopped to think about it lately? Jesus loves me. When we say He loves us, it is a continual flow of love. It is like a river flowing freely; it doesn't stop. It's not dependent on our actions. It doesn't depend on our love for Him. He loves us both now and forever. He loves us in the past, the present, and the future. His love doesn't stop. Nothing we can do will stop Him from loving us! Isn't that Good News?!

> For I am convinced [and continue to be convinced—beyond any doubt] that neither death, nor life, nor angels, nor principalities, nor things present *and* threatening, nor things to come, nor powers, nor height, nor depth, nor any other created thing, will be able to separate us from the [unlimited] love of God, which is in Christ Jesus our Lord.
>
> (*The Amplified Bible*, Romans 8:38-39)

Making Bread

Have you ever made bread from scratch? It takes time. It's not an easy process. You mix the ingredients and then you use your hands to knead the bread. Kneading bread is an important part of the process. You get your hands in there to do the work. Use the heel of your hands to push into the dough then fold the dough over and over again. Keep working on the dough until it is firmer and ready to set aside to rise. After you bake it in the oven, out comes warm, delicious homemade bread!

We say that God is the potter, and we are the clay. We ask God to shape us into a pleasing vessel for His use. We are like the bread dough that God is shaping and forming for His use. The process may be time consuming and messy, but the outcome is worth it!

God is the potter. You are the clay. Let Him shape you into the image of His Son. Give Him permission to take your life, knead it, and form you until you are pleasing to Him.

> Yet you, Lord, are our Father. We are the clay, you are the potter; we are all the work of your hand.
> (*New International Version*, Isaiah 64:8)

Called by God!

You are called!

An ambassador!

A light on a hill!

Salt of the earth!

Imitator of Christ!

Chosen people!

Vessel of God!

Servant of God!

Child of God!

You are called by God!

In the same way, let your light shine before others, that they may see your good deeds and glorify your Father in heaven.

(*New International Version*, Matthew 5:16)

Note to Self

His mercy is new every morning, every single, solitary morning. His great mercy, His love, His forgiveness, His kindness, and His grace are new and free. They are like a new present. Open the package and experience it today. That brand new never used before mercy and grace. When you see the sunrise, it should remind you that His mercy is new again today. Thank God for His mercy!

It is of the Lord's mercies that we are not consumed, because his compassions fail not. They are new every morning: great is thy faithfulness.

(*King James Version*, Lamentations 3:22-23)

TGIF

Thank God it's Friday!!

Friday is so much closer to the weekend. It's on the verge of Saturday and Sunday. We look forward to it. It means that we are almost done with this week.

So often I am looking forward to things in the future and forgetting to make the most of each day. I should live for today. I shouldn't put so much emphasis on the coming weekend. Thank God it's Friday because I have another day of life to live for Him!

It's the journey that counts. Don't wish your life away waiting for the weekend, vacation, or some important event. Enjoy the days leading up to it. Let us rejoice in each day and be glad in it! Let's make the most of today!

> Teach us to number our days and recognize how few they are; help us to spend them as we should.
>
> (*New Living Translation*, Psalms 90:12)

God's Encouragement

Yesterday I was driving and thinking that it sure was a dreary day. I was just routinely driving to a meeting when all of a sudden, I saw bubbles near my car. Bubbles! In the middle of Main Street, I saw kids' bubbles floating through the air.

I couldn't figure out where they came from or who was blowing them either. Was it a car or maybe an apartment that was up on the second floor nearby? I didn't see anyone blowing bubbles, but there they were right in front of me!

When I saw those bubbles, it lifted my spirit. They reminded me that God wants to encourage us. Even on a cloudy day, God is still God. He is in control. Those bubbles brought hope to me; they brought joy to me. I enjoy the simple things in life, and that was encouraging to me. They made me smile!

I thank God for the little things and the simple things that give us pleasure. Don't you just love it when God reminds you of his love?

> You have let me experience the joys of life and the exquisite pleasures of your own eternal presence.
>
> (*The Living Bible*, Psalms 16:11)

Armed with Truth!

When fear, stress, anxiety, worry, etc. comes knocking at your door, don't answer it. That sounds easy to say, but if someone you didn't want in your home knocked at the door, you wouldn't let them in. If a wild animal tried to get in, you wouldn't let it. You would make sure they didn't get in. You would shut and lock the door. You would do all you could to prevent them from coming in.

There are ways to get rid of the enemy when he brings this against you. Pray out loud. "I rebuke worry (stress, fear, pain, etc.) in Jesus' name. I tell it to go. No weapon or worry that is coming against me can prosper. Worry has no authority over me. I am free from worry and anxiety. God has not given me a spirit of fear, but He has given me a spirit of love, of power, and a sound mind. I tell peace to rule and reign in my heart, emotions, and mind in Jesus' name."

I often sing a song afterward about Jesus or His peace. This brings peace to the situation or me. Listening to worship music or reading and declaring scripture can bring me peace, too. It is another weapon to use against the enemy.

Now you are armed with the truth and with spiritual weapons when this attack comes against you.

Be prepared! Be armed! Be strong in the Lord!

> No weapon that is formed against thee shall prosper; and every tongue that shall rise against thee in judgment thou shalt condemn. This is the heritage of the servants of the Lord, and their righteousness is of me, saith the Lord.
>
> (*King James Version*, Isaiah 54:17)

Be Helpful and Kind

As I remember the tragic day of 9/11 that shocked our nation, what I remember most is the unity as people rallied together to help. Many risked their lives to save others. Many others lost their lives that dreadful day. During that terrible time, I saw a bond of unity within our country like never before! People stopped what they were doing to help and to pray.

What reassures my heart is to see the acts of kindness as people reach out to help the recent hurricane victims! You have seen it on the news. The reporter saving the flag and folding it correctly.

People taking boats and trucks to rescue others that are flooded. Line after line of trucks going south to help. I have seen people risking their own lives to help others. Towns in our area have already sent truckloads of supplies. Joining together to do what we can to help those in need; that is unity. Let's continue to pray and help all that we can. Let keep praying for unity.

We should keep praying for unity and safety for our country. Keep helping! Keep praying!

> How good and pleasant it is when God's people live together in unity!
> (*New International Version*, Psalm 133:1)

God is on My Side

I am more than a conqueror through Christ Jesus.
I have the sword of the spirit and the shield of
faith.
I am not intimidated by this situation.
I will not back down. I rise up boldly and
confidently!
With my armor on, I will go forth victoriously.
I will not cower down. I will not stumble and fall.
I will go forward.
My path is straight. My feet are on solid ground.
I can do all things through Christ which
strengthens me.
I have a strong faith!
God is on my side! Victory is mine!

> I can do all things through Christ
> which strengtheneth me.
>
> (*King James Version*, Philippians,
> 4:13)

More Than Enough

God is the God of more than enough. He gives abundantly beyond what we can even think, ask, hope, or imagine. Don't be satisfied with just a little when God can feed over five thousand people with just a young boy's lunch. He can use Gideon with only three hundred men to defeat an army. He can use David, just a shepherd boy, to defeat a giant.

Our thinking prevents us from expecting more. Our thoughts are not God's thoughts, so we often have low expectations. We limit God because we lack faith. In Philippians 4:19 it says that God will supply all our needs according to His riches in glory. It doesn't say our riches or our righteousness, but it depends on God's supply.

Don't you think that He has a big supply of all that you need?! He is our loving Father. He wants to give you what you need-peace, wisdom, comfort, healing, employment, faith, strength, finances, or salvation. What do you need? Just ask Him and believe.

> Now glory be to God, who by his mighty power at work within us is able to do far more than we would ever dare to ask or even dream of— infinitely beyond our highest prayers, desires, thoughts, or hopes.
> (*The Living Bible*, Ephesians 3:20)

Superheroes

There is a lot of talk about superheroes, but Jesus is the original superhero. He overcame death. He performed miracles. He raised the dead, healed the sick, and He restored sight to the blind, healed the lame and deaf! He walked on water! He calmed the storm! He had compassion for others.

Jesus left Heaven to take on sin and the cross! He left His Father to be obedient unto death! He defeated death, Hell, the grave, and came back to life! For you and me!! Someday when the trumpet sounds, He will come back again to take His bride to Heaven with Him! That is pretty super! My hero! My Lord! My Savior! My Jesus!

I pray that God is your Super Hero. I pray that He heals you, calls you out of darkness, and performs miracles for you and your family. I pray that He restores what the enemy has tried to destroy. I pray that He brings peace in the storm and order to chaos. I pray that He shows you His love for you. Jesus be Savior, Lord, King of Kings, and Lord of Lords in our lives!

From that time forth began Jesus to shew unto his disciples, how that he must go unto Jerusalem, and suffer many things of the elders and chief priests and scribes, and be killed, and be raised again the third day. (*King James Version*, Matthew 16:21)

You are Loved

Do you remember back in grade school when they were choosing teams for PE or recess? The first people picked were always the best players. Maybe you were picked last because you weren't very good. It was humiliating!

Guess what? Jesus chose you to be on His team. Each and everyone one of you, He chose you! He looked around and said I want her/him to be on my team!!

You are chosen. You are loved. You are wanted. You are important. You are needed on His team. Let's put our hands together and yell, "Team Jesus"!!

> But you are a chosen people, a royal priesthood, a holy nation, God's special possession, that you may declare the praises of him who called you out of darkness into his wonderful light.
>
> (*New International Version*, 1 Peter 2:9)

In God I am Strong

Sometimes I feel weak in my spirit. I feel discouraged or disappointed. I feel overwhelmed. When that happens, I want to just go to bed and hide under the covers. I want to get away from it all and just stay in my house, but I can't.

Instead, I run to God. God gives me the strength that I need. He gives me the support that I need. When I am weak, He is strong. With the Lord's help, you can withstand anything coming against you. He gives us strength. When we are weak, He is our solid foundation. He is our Rock!

Trust God! Stand strong! A force against you will not bend you! A pressure attacking you will not break you! God's grace will bring breakthrough!

Have not I commanded thee? Be strong and of a good courage; be not afraid, neither be thou dismayed: for the Lord thy God is with thee whithersoever thou goest.

(*King James Version*, Joshua 1:9)

Push Through

I see some of you standing at a door ready to go through, but fear is blocking your way. Fear is like a big bully! It will try to intimidate you and hold you captive. It is like a ball and chain around your ankle. It is meant to prevent you from doing God's will.

If you're dreaming of doing something, don't let fear hold you back. Think of a door in front of you and the sign says push. Push fear right out of the way! Have faith. Go through that door and follow your heart!

> Ask and it will be given to you; seek and you will find; knock and the door will be opened to you. For everyone who asks receives; the one who seeks finds; and to the one who knocks, the door will be opened.
>
> (*New International Version*, Matthew 7:7-8)

New Possibilities!

I woke up and stretched to greet the new day!
My face turned toward Heaven.
Immediately I started thanking God!
Praises to God filled my mind.
My thoughts were filled with thanksgiving, hope,
and promise for this day.
A new day!
A new beginning!
New possibilities!

Guide me in your truth and teach me, for you are God my Savior, and my hope is in you all day long.

(*New International Version*, Psalm 25:5)

What a Difference Jesus Makes!

Have you seen those tests on TV comparing one brand of detergent to another? They take two dirty white shirts with stains and wash them in two different detergents then compare the two to see which one works the best.

If you compared my life before and after I knew God and invited Jesus into my heart, the difference is extraordinary. The changes in my life are as evident as those white shirts that came out super clean. It is easy to see the difference. Without Jesus, I would be lost, but now I am found.

I am so thankful for my salvation. It has changed my life and continues to do so! He is transforming us into the image of His Son. He has forgiven us, cleansed us, and made us white as snow!

Neither is there salvation in any other: for there is none other name under heaven given among men, whereby we must be saved.

(*King James Version*, Acts 4:12)

Light of the World

In the dark night, a sliver of light from the
crescent moon shone forth. The sphere of the
moon was just a dull outline. It was odd that the
whole moon wasn't shining brighter letting the
sun shine through it. I wonder, do I have a sliver
of God that shines out of me, or am I dull like the
crescent moon?

Ask Him to let His love shine brightly out of you.
Ask Him to help you walk in love, compassion,
and mercy towards others. Live your life for Him.

You are the light of the world. A town built on a
hill cannot be hidden. Neither do people light a
lamp and put it under a bowl. Instead they put
it on its stand, and it gives light to everyone in
the house. In the same way, let your light shine
before others, that they may see your good
deeds and glorify your Father in heaven.

(*New International Version*, Matthew 5:14-16)

Hold Fast!

I won't look at the mountain before. I won't be overwhelmed or confused. I will wait! I will stand strong!

Until God changes things, answers prayer, or intervenes, I will believe God!

I will not give in or give up! I will believe Him! I will hold fast to Him, His Word, and promises.

Until God shows up, I will believe!!

> But you are to hold fast to the Lord your God, as you have until now.
>
> (*New International Version*, Joshua 23:8)

Say this out loud!

I am...

Loved!

Saved!

Forgiven!

Blessed!

Righteous!

Redeemed!

Victorious!

A child of God!

A woman/man of faith!

> For whatsoever is born of God overcometh the world: and this is the victory that overcometh the world, even our faith. Who is he that overcometh the world, but he that believeth that Jesus is the Son of God?
>
> (*King James Version*, 1 John 5:4-5)

The Greatest Commandment

One of the most basic but deep prayers that I pray is just two verses from the Bible. If we can do this,I think it will motivate us to do what is right, to obey God, to spend more time with Him in prayer, seek Him, to grow spiritually, and to love others. Heeding the words of Jesus will cause us to be more like Him as we live for Him.

What is this passionate prayer you ask? It is the greatest commandment! It is written four times in the Bible in Matthew, Mark, Luke, and Deuteronomy. We should love God then others. That is a deep prayer to pray: for a love with all your heart, with all your soul, with all your mind, and with all your strength! Only God can love like that, but I keep praying that my love will increase.

All we need is to love God with our whole being, and it will change our lives and others!

The words of Jesus say, "Love the Lord your God with all your heart and with all your soul and with all your mind and with all your strength.' The second is this: 'Love your neighbor as yourself.' There is no commandment greater than these." (New International Version, Mark 12:30-31)

God Loves Me!

I am so thankful that I know and love God. What's really awesome is that He knows and loves me!! Me-just a speck of dirt on this planet of billions of people! In all the galaxies of the universe, He knows me.

I am barely a dot on this earth, and God knows my name. He knows the number of hairs on my head. He knows my thoughts, my hopes, my dreams, and my future. He knows my failures, mistakes, and sin. He has forgiven me and saved me. He has a plan for my life.

In a group of billions of people, He can point us out and call us by name! He loves us very much! I am so grateful for His love!!

> For God so loved the world, that he gave his only begotten Son, that whosoever believeth in him should not perish, but have everlasting life.
>
> (*King James Version*, John 3:16)

Risen Savior

A crown of thorns! A robe!

A sign that said the King of the Jews!

Forsaken! Beaten!

A crucified, innocent man!

Beloved Son! Sacrificial lamb!

A risen Savior! Jesus, my Lord!

Resurrection Sunday!

For what I received I passed on to you as of first
importance: that Christ died for our sins
according to the Scriptures,
that he was buried, that he was raised on the
third day according to the Scriptures.

(*King James Version,* 1 Corinthians 15:3-4)

Let the River Flow!

You've heard of people swimming with dolphins. I had a friend come to my class to tell the students about her experience. This was before it was a popular thing to do. The students were so interested. She showed them her pictures, and she explained that she got right in the water with them. She wasn't afraid at all. She held onto one as it pulled her around the pool like she was going for a ride. She truly enjoyed the experience!

In Ezekiel 47, it speaks of the river of God. To me, the river is like the Holy Spirit. This passage encourages us to get into the deep with God and not be satisfied with just a little.

Immerse yourself completely in the things of God. Seek Him with all your heart. Swim with God and let Him guide your life. When you do that, the river will flow with abundant life, love, joy, peace, faith, and purpose like you have never experienced before. Let the River flow!

And it shall come to pass, that every thing that liveth, which moveth, whithersoever the rivers shall come, shall live: and there shall be a very great multitude of fish, because these waters shall come thither: for they shall be healed; and everything shall live whither the river cometh.

(*King James Version*, Ezekiel 47:9)

Pray and Believe!

Chasing after Moses and the Israelites was Pharaoh's army. Right in front of them was the sea. Now, what did they do?

When the enemy is at your back and a mountain in front of you, what do you do? When you are closed in by your circumstances, or when you can't see the end result, what do you do? Are you afraid? Do you complain or give up? Or, do you pray, have faith, and believe that God will show up?

Turn to God in prayer. He will hear and answer you. He will make a way. A clear path will be exposed for you to cross through. The water will be pushed out of the way so you can go through on dry land. Don't give up, but believe that God is going to show up! Have faith!

Some trust in chariots and some in horses, but we trust in the name of the Lord our God.

(*New International Version*, Psalms 20:7)

Walk in Joy

Just like we need three meals a day, we need God in our lives all day long. Let's put Jesus first. Think about Him, serve Him, love Him, and praise Him. See if that doesn't change your attitude. When you continue to look to Jesus, it will bring joy! That's a good way to start the day!

Walk in joy to enjoy life!

The Lord is my strength and my shield; my heart trusts in him, and he helps me. My heart leaps for joy, and with my song I praise him.

(*New International Version*, Psalms 28:7)

Perspective

In school, we were talking about the point of view or the author's perspective when he writes a book. We were noticing the differences of a story and when a different character tells the same story.

The students told me that many of their video games have the choice of the point of view. If they click on the first-person point of view, they see the game through their own eyes like they are the main character. If they choose third person point of view, they watch someone else's story. Of course, they really like the first-person point of view best because they get to experience it.

This reminds me of the quote, "Don't judge a person until you've walked a mile in their shoes." We really have no idea what another person is going through unless we have gone through it, too. Most times even walking through the same kind of battle is still not the same.

Let's try seeing someone else's perspective. Try to see both sides of a situation. Let's not judge others; instead, let's be kind, give an encouraging word, or pray for them.

Let's look at it through our own eyes and walk in compassion and mercy. After all, that's what God has done for us.

Go spread kindness!

And be ye kind one to another, tenderhearted, forgiving one another, even as God for Christ's sake hath forgiven you.

(*The Living Bible*, Ephesians 4:32)

Set your Sights on Jesus!

You have heard that life is a journey. To go on a journey, you must know the way. You set the navigation on your car. At first, you enjoy the ride. Everything is going fine. You laugh, see the sights, stay on track, but then the road gets hilly, with unexpected twists and turns. The nice enjoyable ride becomes a white-knuckled grip on the steering wheel. You slow down to navigate the turns. Your focus turns towards just staying on the road. It can be difficult, but you keep your focus. You pray. You trust God. You know that you are on track. The journey is not what you had expected, but you can do it because your focus is on Jesus. You get your eyes off the problems and get your eyes on Jesus. He is your navigator.

Life is not always easy. But you have to trust your navigator. As long as you stay on track, His track, then you will make it to the right destination. Each day set your sights on the prize! Focus on Jesus! Let Him be your navigator.

> And let us run with perseverance the race marked out for us, fixing our eyes on Jesus, the pioneer and perfecter of faith. For the joy set before him he endured the cross, scorning its shame, and sat down at the right hand of the throne of God. Consider him who endured such opposition from sinners, so that you will not grow weary and lose heart.
> (*New International Version*, Hebrews 12:1-3

Hold on to The Word

Anytime I have had to have a procedure done, I read Psalm 62:1-2. Even on the way to the hospital when fear is trying to creep in, I declare these verses. It calms me. It brings me peace of mind. The word always encourages me. It is my stability in the storm. It is like a life preserver. I cling to it, and it keeps me afloat.

What is bombarding you? Get in the scripture and find a verse to calm you or encourage you. The Word of God will bring you peace, strength, wisdom, or whatever you need no matter what you are going through. Read it! Declare it! Pray it! Hold on to it tightly. Never let it go, and you will find God!!

Truly my soul finds rest in God; my salvation comes from him. Truly he is my rock and my salvation; he is my fortress, I will never be shaken.

(*New International Version,* Psalm 62:1-2)

Go Boldly

"Not by might nor by power but by the spirit," says the Lord. We noticed this when David faced the Goliath. David did not have might or strength of his own to fight a giant. He was just a teen and not even in the army. He had no power of his own. He went alone to fight, but he wasn't alone. He went in the name of the Lord. The Spirit of God led him to face Goliath, and by the Spirit, David defeated him.

When you feel you lack might, power, energy, confidence, or strength, know the Spirit of God is with you! You can boldly face your giant and gain victory!

> Then he answered and spake unto me, saying, This is the word of the Lord unto Zerubbabel, saying, Not by might, nor by power, but by my spirit, saith the Lord of hosts.
>
> (*King James Version*, Zechariah 4:6)

Wait on the Lord

Be patient when you have prayed about something. God's timing is not our timing. We may have prayed about it for many days, months, or years. You may have believed for a long time. Don't give up just yet because your miracle may be just around the corner.

The hardest time to wait on the Lord is usually right before He sends the answer. Be strong and of good courage. Have faith that help will arrive at just the right time!

Wait on the Lord: be of good courage, and he shall strengthen thine heart: wait, I say, on the Lord.

(*King James Version*, Psalm 27:14)

Special Delivery

Fearfully and wonderfully made.
Made with love.
Made in the image of God.

Unique and special.
God's masterpiece.

Look at the name tag.
It says your name!

You are God's special creation!
Made with love!

He created you.
You were on His mind!
Your Father loves you!

For we are God's masterpiece. He has created us anew in Christ Jesus, so we can do the good things he planned for us long ago.
(*New Life Version*, Ephesians 2:10)

God will Provide

Today is my payday. I can't help but be grateful to God for His provision. Throughout the years, there have been times when we really struggled. We didn't have much money or even have a job, but God was always faithful.

We have lived through difficult times, but God has provided each and every time. I am so thankful to God! You may be having a tough time right now. Just remember that God will provide. He is faithful!

> But my God shall supply all your needs according to his riches in glory by Christ Jesus.
>
> (*King James Version*, Philippians 4:19)

Calm in Your Chaos

In the midst of a busy day, take five minutes to stop and just focus on God. Say a quick prayer, say a verse, praise Him, and refocus your thoughts. Zero in on God and totally pull away from the hustle and bustle of the day. See if this doesn't calm you.

Jesus is the center of your life. Bring Him right there in the center of your day. See what happens. Watch Jesus show up!

Be careful for nothing; but in everything by prayer and supplication with thanksgiving let your requests be made known unto God.

(*King James Version*, Philippians 4:6)

Uniquely You

Each one of you is unique and made by God. He created all your parts and put you together in your mother's womb. He not only created your DNA, appearance, and personality, but He created your gifts and talents to be used especially for His Glory.

You are a work of art, God's masterpiece. You were created by a loving Father to stand out not fade into the background. Take your place in this world! Be in the world, but not of the world! Don't be a wallflower. Be the unique person that God created you to be!

> For we are God's masterpiece. He has created us anew in Christ Jesus, so we can do the good things he planned for us long ago.
>
> (*New Living Translation,* Ephesians 2:10)

Stay the Course

Have you ever noticed how surfers ride the waves? It looks easy, but it's not. The purpose of surfing is to ride the waves and to enjoy the ride and the challenge. Surfers continue to work to get better at their sport day after day. Occasionally, they will fall off the board, but then get back up and try again.

This reminds me of life. Life is full of challenges. Storms rise up and knock us off the board. But we have to get back up when we fall off, mess up, or get sidetracked.

If you have wiped out, it's time to get back up on that board and start riding the waves again! Stay the course! Enjoy the ride! Meet the challenge! You can do this! Remember, God is with us!

> Now may our Lord Jesus Christ Himself and God our Father, who has loved us and given us everlasting comfort and encouragement and the good [well-founded] hope [of salvation] by His grace, comfort and encourage and strengthen your hearts [keeping them steadfast and on course] in every good work and word.
> (*The Amplified Version*,
> 2 Thessalonians 2:16-17)

God's Beauty

God created the Earth and all that is in it. He created the changing seasons. Autumn is so beautiful with the vibrant colors of the leaves. It is like a beautiful painting. There is a little chill in the air, but it is not too cold yet. When the sun is shining, it is so brilliant.

God made all this beauty, all this majesty, all this brilliance, and all the colors in nature. He paints this majestic work of art in nature because He is majestic. He is the master artist creating this breathtaking painting for all to enjoy.

Enjoy God's beauty. It is free! Just look out your window or step outside! It's awesome! It's magnificent! It reveals God!

> And God said, Let there be lights in the firmament of the heaven to divide the day from the night; and let them be for signs, and for seasons, and for days, and years: And let them be for lights in the firmament of the heaven to give light upon the earth: and it was so.
>
> (*King James Version*, Genesis 1:14-15)

Snuggle In

There's nothing like the comfortable feeling of getting into my bed at night. As I put my legs in, I feel the soft, clean sheets. I lay my head down on my soft pillows and then spread out on my comfortable bed. Pulling the quilts up over me makes me feel safe and secure. I feel warm in my cocoon of protection that is spread over me. I snuggle in until I get into the right position, then I quiet my soul to rest. Oh, the cozy feeling!!

I am so thankful for my position in Christ Jesus. It is like resting in my comfortable bed. I am safe and secure. I am seated in heavenly places-a place of rest and confidence, a place of peace, a refuge in times of trouble, a place of joy. I am surrounded by God's favor as a shield about me. He is my refuge and strength. He has spread his protection and His righteousness over me. I am covered by His love. Oh, the cozy feeling!!

But let all who take refuge in you be glad; let them ever sing for joy. Spread your protection over them, that those who love your name may rejoice in you. Surely, Lord, you bless the righteous; you surround them with your favor as with a shield.

(*New International Version*, Psalm 5:11-12)

Don't Give Up! Trust God!

Some of you have been bombarded with physical problems, but you have stood your ground and kept on going in His power and His strength. Overcomer!

Some of you are going through a difficult situation, but you are depending on God. He can make a way where there seems to be no way. Overcomer!

Some of you have been through a difficult trial, but you didn't fall down or give up. God is your refuge and strength in times of trouble. Overcomer!

Some of you have struggled with debt and lack of finances, but you know God will meet all your needs according to His riches in glory. Overcomer!

Some of you have gotten a bad report, but you aren't giving in to fear. You are trusting God. Overcomer!

Some of you have lost a close family member, but heartache and tears didn't stop you from going on with God. Overcomer!

Some of you are tired of the struggle. In your weakness God is strong. You can do all things through Christ which strengthens you. Overcomer!

Some of you are overwhelmed and stressed, but God is your anchor in the storm. Overcomer!

You are an overcomer through Christ Jesus our Lord! Overcoming whatever comes against you with God! You are strong! You are trusting God. You are an overcomer!

> For whatsoever is born of God overcometh the world: and this is the victory that overcometh the world, even our faith. Who is he that overcometh the world, but he that believeth that Jesus is the Son of God?
> (*King James Version,* 1 John 5:4-5)

My Help

Not only does my help come from the Lord, but so does my strength, my peace, my healing, my wisdom, my comfort, my guidance, my salvation, my provision, my courage, my blessings, my faith, and my hope. He is all that I need.

If I need peace, I will ask Him for it. If I need hope, I seek God. If I need wisdom, I pray for it. If I need help, I will ask God. If I need strength, I get it from God. God has all that I need. He is the Lord God, maker of heaven and earth. Look to the Lord. He has all you need. What do you need today? Ask God!

> My help cometh from the Lord, which made heaven and earth.
>
> (*King James Version*, Psalm 121:2)

Don't Let Go

If God has given you a dream or a promise, don't let anyone tell you that it can't be done or it won't happen. Several years ago, I started writing books like this one after months of praying about it and asking people if they would even read it. One night I felt compelled to do it. Without hesitation, believing that God had called me to do encourage believers, I just did it.

If God is compelling you to do something, do it. Don't hesitate. Follow God. Don't be hindered by doubt or fear. Don't be held back by what other people think. Just do it. Step out of the boat and see what happens. Go forth in faith. God will be with you every step of the way.

> Now unto him that is able to do exceeding abundantly above all that we ask or think, according to the power that worketh in us.
>
> (*King James Version*, Ephesians 3:20)

Do Not be Afraid

When you are going through a difficult time, remember the Israelites walking on dry ground through the Red Sea. Walls of water pushed up away from the ground so they could walk on through. Pharaoh and his army were still coming. It was still tense and frightening, but God- He showed up and provided a miracle!

When you are going through a tough time-pray! When we pray, we are praying to the life-giving, miracle-working, way-making, Almighty God, our Father!! Don't look behind you at the circumstances. Look to God! Know that He is at work, He provides, and He is faithful!

Moses answered the people, "Do not be afraid. Stand firm and you will see the deliverance the Lord will bring you today. The Egyptians you see today you will never see again. The Lord will fight for you; you need only to be still."

(*New International Version*, Exodus 14:13-14)

Let it Go!

Some people hold onto their burdens. Some hold on to unforgiveness. We hold on tight and can't let go of it. We often lug it around on our shoulders like a heavy backpack. It gets heavier and heavier the more we carry it. It starts weighing us down. We are not supposed to carry it around. We should give it to God. Let go of it once and for all.

Cast all your cares on Him because He cares for you. If you are worried, then you haven't given it to God. Let it go!! If you are holding on to unforgiveness, let it go! If you are overwhelmed, let it go! If you are stressed, let it go! If you have the cares of the world on your shoulders, let it go!! Give it to God. Let it go once and for all!

Casting all your care upon him;
for he careth for you.

(*King James Version*, 1 Peter 5:7)

Seek Jesus

Today I will do it. I will go after this Jesus that I have heard heals people. Either that or lay here and die. I have to do this because my life depends on it.

Leaving the safety of my home is scary! Each step hurts and is difficult for me. Out of breath, I stop to lean on a building. I have to keep going forward. I must find Him.

I see a crowd up ahead. There He is in the middle of the crowd. How will I ever get to Him? When He stops to talk, I will gather all my strength and walk towards Him.

Pushing my way through the crowd, I almost get knocked down. I am so close. If I could just touch Him... I stretch out my hand to touch Him but only touch the hem of his cloak. A warmth feeling runs through my body. Strength returns to me. I haven't felt like this in twelve years. I feel restored and alive again.

Jesus turns around asking who touched Him. I try to hide in the crowd, but He insists that someone touched Him. I fall before Him thankful for my healing. Jesus looks at me and says to me, " your faith has made me whole. Go in peace."

The heaviness is gone, and I am full of joy and strength! I feel whole, I feel well, I feel peace. My Jesus-healer, deliverer, restorer. My Savior!

Be determined just like this woman.
Pursue Jesus! Seek Him! Find Him!

> Then the woman, seeing that she could not go unnoticed, came trembling and fell at his feet. In the presence of all the people, she told why she had touched him and how she had been instantly healed. Then he said to her, "Daughter, your faith has healed you. Go in peace."
>
> (*New International Version*, Luke 8:47-48)

He Loves You

Have you ever accidentally eavesdropped on a conversation? I overheard this conversation, and I wanted to tell you what I heard. He was looking very serious discussing love. He was saying that you are loved. He loves you so much that you don't even realize the magnitude of his love for you. God's thoughts are not our thoughts, and His ways are not our ways. It is hard to fathom the depth of His love. The kind of love that lays down His life for another. The love that took up the cross. Love that surpasses all worldly love.

Then with tears in His eyes, He said you are His own dearly loved child. He loves you with an everlasting love. The love of the Father is so deep, so strong, so forgiving, so dear, so loving, and so wide. We are loved. Then He looked up at me and smiled and said, "Go ahead and tell them. They need to know this." Then He paused and said, "I really do love you!"

> For God so loved the world, that he gave his only begotten Son, that whosoever believeth in him should not perish, but have everlasting life.
>
> (*King James Version*, John 3:16)

Prayer and Praise

In Acts 12, Peter was in jail, and the church was earnestly praying for him. An angel came and set him free from the chains and bondage. In Acts 16, Paul and Silas had been beaten and thrown in jail. In the middle of the night while singing praises, an earthquake broke open the prison doors, and all the chains came loose. They were set free.

We may not be in a physical prison right now, but there can still be things that hold us back and hinder us. These things are strongholds in our lives that prevent us from doing what we are called to do. For example, fear may keep you from going after that dream, changing a job, doing the right thing, or giving your life to God. Lies may tell you that you can't do it or you are too young or too old. Depression may hold you captive. Your finances may be lacking. Condemnation may be telling you that you aren't good enough or that God can't forgive you. Those are lies of the enemy. Don't let the enemy hold you captive.

How did they get out of prison? Prayer and praise!! Ask God to show you the chains that confine you. Ask Him to set you free. Praise His name. Pray and get others to pray for you! Wait for those chains to fall off. Expect God to show up!

Peter therefore was kept in prison: but prayer was made without ceasing of the church unto God for him.

(*King James Version*, Acts 12:5)

He Calls Your Name

I sat wide-eyed staring at the television. I was only four or five years old, but I didn't want to miss my favorite TV show. At the closing of the show, the lady would pretend to look through a magic mirror to see all the children that were watching. Then she would call out children's names. She'd say, "I see Bobby and Carol and Lisa and Mark. I see Jill and Frank and Terri and Jack."

I continued to watch it faithfully, eager to hear my name called. I sat up straight listening intently week after week. I always wanted to hear my name, but I never did.

You don't have to wait for someone to call your name. God already has. He has called each of us by name. He calls us his precious daughters and sons. He created you! He loves you! Be happy that God calls your name! You are dearly loved!

But now thus saith the Lord that created thee, O Jacob, and he that formed thee, O Israel, Fear not: for I have redeemed thee, I have called thee by thy name; thou art mine.

(*King James Version*, Isaiah 43:1)

Keep on Going!

Have you seen the people cheering on runners on the sidelines of a race? Sometimes they hold up signs to encourage them. As they run by, people are clapping, encouraging, yelling, and shaking their signs to encourages them to keep going. It gives them a boost when they are weary. They get a second wind and continue on stronger than before.

Imagine a stretch of road. There are people lined up on both sides cheering you on. You are the one running the race. You are the one winning. People are yelling for you. They are encouraging you. They want you to keep going. There is a sign that says, "I can do all things through Christ which strengthens me."

Be encouraged. Don't give up. Keep on going! With God all things are possible! Get a second wind and continue on stronger than before in this race we call life!

Wherefore seeing we also are compassed about with so great a cloud of witnesses, let us lay aside every weight, and the sin which doth so easily beset us, and let us run with patience the race that is set before us, Looking unto Jesus the author and finisher of our faith.

(*King James Version*, Hebrews 12:1-2a)

Seek God

I seek God much more during a rough time than when I am on the mountaintop. I walk closer and try to hear Him even more. I want to know every step that I should take. I want to feel His presence and comfort, so I run to Him and feel safe. He is my refuge.

When I am out of the storm, I am so thankful, but then I forget that I need Him. I start thinking that I can do it alone. I am like a baby starting to walk. Let go of me, and let me be independent until I need you. I have to learn to depend on Him more and not let go. I need Him whether I am feeling great or having a rough day.

No matter what the season, God will see us through if we seek Him, trust Him, and do not depend on ourselves. Have faith in God. Trust Him at all times!

Trust in him at all times; ye people, pour out your heart before him: God is a refuge for us. Selah.

(*King James Version*, Psalm 62:8)

Making Memories

Do you remember tracing your hand to make a turkey? Your thumb was the head. You put eyes and a mouth on it. Then, the other fingers were the feathers. It was easy, fast, and fun to make.

Do you remember making turkeys with construction paper feathers? Each feather was a different color (those were colorful turkeys), and you wrote what you were thankful for on each feather. Sometimes the whole class made one big turkey with twenty or more feathers. One for each student.

Memories and being thankful are part of this season. I hope that you have good memories and make new ones this year. Let us give thanks with a grateful heart to God.

Give thanks to the Lord, for he is good; his love endures forever.

(*New International Version,* 2 Chronicles 16:34)

Uniquely Made

We have to remind our self that not only are we a child of the Most High God, but we are created uniquely by Him. We are different, and there is a reason for our differences.

God created us this way so we can be used by Him. We are unique in our personality and talents. We shouldn't try to be like anyone else. Like the snowflake, we are all uniquely made and beautiful to Him. We are created by God our Father with the utmost care and love.

For we are his workmanship, created in Christ Jesus unto good works, which God hath before ordained that we should walk in them.

(King James Version, Ephesians 2:10)

Hope and a Future

Remember when you were young, and you always wanted to be older. You dreamed about your future. You dreamed about life. You dreamed about driving a car, getting married, and going to college. You looked forward to your future years. God has hope and a future for you. No matter what age! You haven't missed it. Stay on track. Take that step of faith! He will use you no matter what your age. He has a hope and a future for you!

> "For I know the plans I have for you," declares the Lord, "plans to prosper you and not to harm you, plans to give you hope and a future."
>
> (*New International Version,* Jeremiah 29:11)

Mercy and Grace

Mercy is when someone extends forgiveness and kindness to you. God's mercy is His forgiveness and kindness extended to us when we don't deserve it. I am thankful to God for His mercy.

When I think of mercy and forgiveness, I picture a chalkboard in my mind with all my sin and mess ups written on it. Then I see a loving Father wipe it all clean because of the blood of Jesus. He forgives it all and cleanses me. He makes me white as snow. Thank God for His mercy!

> Come now, and let us reason together, saith the Lord: though your sins be as scarlet, they shall be as white as snow; though they be red like crimson, they shall be as wool.
>
> (*King James Version*, Isaiah 1:18)

Hunger for Him

I went to the grocery store one day and bought groceries for the week. Later that evening, I was looking for something to eat. I couldn't find anything even though the cabinets were full. I said that there was nothing to eat. There really was a lot to eat, but it wasn't what I wanted. There was nothing that would satisfy my hunger.

Wouldn't it be great if that was the kind of hunger that we had for Jesus?! Look all around at what could satisfy your soul and know that Jesus is the only answer. He is what you are craving. He is what you need. He is the longing of your hunger.

Don't try to fill up with leftovers from yesterday, junk food, or empty calories. Don't be satisfied until you've tasted and seen that He is good. He is all that will satisfy your soul. Seek Him, and you will find Him.

O taste and see that the Lord is good: blessed is the man that trusteth in him.

(*King James Version*, Psalm 34:8)

Share with Others

Let us share with others. It could make a difference in someone's life today. A kind word, a monetary gift, a helpful hand, a prayer, or a hug to someone in need can encourage them. You can make a difference one person at a time or one day at a time. Imagine the impact you could have!

What if we all do this? Imagine what a great place this world would be. Plus, it is rewarding and satisfying to give. Christmas is wonderful season to give to others, but every day is a great day to show the love of Jesus. Give!

> Give, and it will be given to you. A good measure, pressed down, shaken together and running over, will be poured into your lap. For with the measure you use, it will be measured to you."
>
> (*New International Version,* Luke 6:38)

God is Faithful

This verse reminds me of God's faithfulness.

He is the God who was. He was faithful in my life in my past. I can look back on the past and see how he brought me through. I remember the answers to prayer, the opportunities, the praise reports, and the victories. It encourages me. He was faithful!

He is present now. He is in my life right now. I know that He will bring me through this day, this hour, and this minute. He is here with me. He is faithful!

He is to come. He is my future. He will not leave me nor forsake me. He is always with me and will continue to be with me. My future is secure in him. I remember how God brought me through in the past and the present. I see his faithfulness in my future. He has been with me every step of the way. Confidently, I can face today, this week, and this season!!

> Holy, holy, holy, is the Lord God Almighty, who was, and is, and is to come.
>
> (*New International Version*, Revelation 4:8b)

Work in Progress

Have you heard the statement that God is working on me? He's not through with me yet. Isn't that the truth?!

I am grateful that He is at work in me. He hasn't given up on me. He hasn't stopped supporting me and encouraging me. He sees and knows what I can do. He believes in me when others don't. He believes in me when I don't even believe in myself. He will cheer me on to the finish line because He knows what I am capable of doing through Him. No telling what we can accomplish through Him if we keep going!

Keep working on me, Lord. I am a work in progress!!

Being confident of this very thing, that he which hath begun a good work in you will perform it until the day of Jesus Christ.

(*King James Version*, Philippians 1:6)

Amazing Love

What amazing love God has for us! For God so loved the world. He so very dearly loved the people of the world. He loves us-you and I- so much that He willingly gave His Son, Jesus. He gave His dearly loved Son so that we could have a relationship with Him. He gave Jesus to the world which hated Him in order for us to be set free from sin and death.

God loved us so much that He gave His Son. He gave so that we could receive salvation and eternal life. He gave so that we would be able to live life with Him if we choose. That's an amazing love!

God so loved the world that he gave his one and only Son, that whoever believes in him shall not perish but have eternal life.

(*New International Version,* John 3:16)

Follow Him!

Moses was leading the Israelites out of Egypt in Exodus 13 and 14. As they left Egypt, the Red Sea was before them and the Egyptian army behind them. It seemed as if they were surrounded, but God was with them. He was their cloud by day and fire by night. He never left them. He appointed Moses to lead them out of slavery to the promised land. All they had to do was follow him.

God goes before us. He is our rear guard. He never leaves us. He is our leader. All we have to do is follow Him, then we will see our promised land and our victory! Follow Him!!

But he said, Yea rather, blessed are they that hear the word of God, and keep it.

(King James Version, Luke 11:28)

Give it to God

Have you seen the heavy backpacks that students carry to school? Since they are full of books, they are very heavy. They are too full and weigh the students down. Sometimes students want to carry all their books to class instead of going to their lockers. That makes for a heavy load.

Sometimes we are carrying a heavy load around, too. We have the weight of the world on our shoulders, but God doesn't want us to carry it. He wants to take it from us. Scripture says to cast your cares on Him because He cares for you. *The Amplified Bible* says to "cast your anxieties, your worries, and your concerns" on Him.

God doesn't want us to be burdened down. Give your cares to the Lord. You don't have to carry them any longer. You don't have to hold on to them. When you give it to God, it's like giving Him a heavy backpack full of textbooks to carry. You will feel the weight lifted off your shoulders. Give it to Him. He cares for you, He loves you, and He wants the best for you! Don't walk around with the heaviness; give it to God!

Casting all your care upon him;
for he careth for you.

(King James Version, 1 Peter 5:7)

God Loves You

God loves you. He is your Father. He loves you more than you can imagine. He loves you much more than any earthly Father or parent. He loves you more than the bridegroom loves the bride. He loves you more than you can fathom.

No matter what, He loves you. He never stops loving you. You are precious to Him. You are loved with a love so deep, so wide, so strong, and so high that you can never know the depths of it. You will always be loved by God. It is an everlasting love from your Father God.

> For I am persuaded, that neither death, nor life, nor angels, nor principalities, nor powers, nor things present, nor things to come, nor height, nor depth, nor any other creature, shall be able to separate us from the love of God, which is in Christ Jesus our Lord.
>
> (*King James Version*, Romans 8:38-39)

Salvation

You know when you see or hear something that seems too good to be true that you get skeptical. You know that there is a catch. We are all looking for that good deal. I like a good deal myself.

Salvation may seem too good to be true, but it's not! Salvation is free. All you have to do is invite Jesus into your heart. The love of your Heavenly Father is freely given to you. Ask and you will receive his mercy, grace, forgiveness, salvation, and eternal life.

We have been given the gift of salvation because Jesus paid for our sin. Jesus did it all. All you have to do is ask Him to forgive you and invite Him into your heart and life. Then you get to spend eternity with God if you believe in Jesus. It's that simple. Now that seems like a deal too good to be true, but it's not! The gift of God is eternal life through Jesus Christ our Lord. Have you asked Jesus into your heart?

> That if thou shalt confess with thy mouth the Lord Jesus, and shalt believe in thine heart that God hath raised him from the dead, thou shalt be saved. For with the heart man believeth unto righteousness; and with the mouth confession is made unto salvation.
> (*King James Version,* Romans 10:9-10)

Peace Touch

Remember playing tag when you were young! It was always so much fun to run and play. I tried hard to stay far away from the person that was it. I didn't want to be it. I would try to hide or stay far away.

Wouldn't it be better if we played a good game of tag where you tagged people with peace? The Peace Touch?! Taking peace with us wherever we go and pass it on like a game of tag spreading it to others. We could pass on the peace of God. I am tagging you with the Peace Touch. Tag, you are it! Pass it on!!

> Blessed are the peacemakers, for they will be called children of God.
>
> *(King James Version,* Matthew 5:9)

The Way!

The crowd is too big! The door is blocked. They can't get in through the windows either. There is no way to get to Him. They are desperately seeking a way in, but the only way left is the roof. It will take some strategizing and a little work to get the roof opened up and the man up there, but there is no other way. Finally, they lower their friend down through the roof right in front of Jesus.

That's what I call determination. A blocked door, a crowded room, or a roof will not prevent them from seeking and finding Jesus. No roadblock was too great. They were pursuing Him. They must get him to Jesus. It was worth the difficulties because their friend was forgiven and healed!!

Life is full of difficulties, but press on. If you are facing a closed door, a roadblock, or a difficulty, seek God. He will point the way to the answer. He will make a way. Have faith! He will show you the way. He is the way! Diligently seek Him!

> And when they could not find by what way they might bring him in because of the multitude, they went upon the housetop, and let him down through the tiling with his couch into the midst before Jesus.
>
> (*New International Version,* Luke 5:19-19)

Come in

"My door is always open." You have heard people say that sometimes. God says his door is always open to us, too. In Hebrews, it says that we can come before our God boldly and confidently.

Just like Esther came before the king and he received her. She wasn't turned away, but she found favor before him. He told her to draw near to him. God receives us just like that, and we receive favor, too. He wants us to come before Him in prayer and worship. His door is open, step on through. He has listening ears, forgiveness, peace, answers, wisdom, grace, mercy, favor, and salvation for you.

> Let us therefore come boldly unto the throne of grace, that we may obtain mercy, and find grace to help in time of need.
>
> (*King James Version,* Hebrews 4:16)

Don't Give Up!

Don't give up!
You can do this!
Don't quit!
Don't give up or give in!
Fix your eyes on Jesus!
Be strong. Be courageous!
The Lord your God is with you!

Therefore, since we are surrounded by such a great cloud of witnesses, let us throw off everything that hinders and the sin that so easily entangles. And let us run with perseverance the race marked out for us, fixing our eyes on Jesus, the pioneer and perfecter of faith.

(*New International Version,* Hebrews 12:1-2)

Goals

I was lost. I didn't know what to do. It was before we had navigation systems in our cars or on our phones. I called someone, and they looked up what I should do. Eventually, I just turned around and went back to my missed exit. I wish I had a GPS back then because it would have kept me on track and helped me not waste time.

A GPS is supposed to map your destination. It's good to map out your goals or destination for your life or the new year. Reflect back on what you've accomplished or wanted to accomplish. Make changes if necessary.

Sometimes we have to make adjustments if we get off track. I want to do what God wants this year not what I want. What do you want to accomplish for God? Are you on the right track? Are you getting closer to your goal?

Let God navigate your life whether it's at this minute, this day, or this year. Let Him show you what He wants you to accomplish.

> "Friends, don't get me wrong: By no means do I count myself an expert in all of this, but I've got my eye on the goal, where God is beckoning us onward—to Jesus. I'm off and running, and I'm not turning back.

So let's keep focused on that goal, those of us who want everything God has for us. If any of you have something else in mind, something less than total commitment, God will clear your blurred vision—you'll see it yet! Now that we're on the right track, let's stay on it."
(*The Message Bible*, Philippians 3:14-16)

God Will Move

Even when things look bleak, God will move. Even when you are in the storm, God will move. When darkness surrounds you, God will move.

Even though the Israelites had been enslaved, God moved. God had a plan of salvation in place for Moses to lead the people out of bondage. God moved on their behalf! It looked like they were pinned in on all sides-the river before them and the Egyptian army close behind them. God moved! He miraculously moved the water totally out of the way so that they could walk on dry ground. They were still being pursued by the Egyptian army, but God moved! They were totally delivered!

God will move! Do not be afraid. Wait on it! See the salvation of the Lord. The Lord shall fight for you. Hold on to peace. Go forward with God! See God move!

And Moses said unto the people, Fear ye not, stand still, and see the salvation of the Lord, which he will shew to you to day: for the Egyptians whom ye have seen today, ye shall see them again no more forever. The Lord shall fight for you, and ye shall hold your peace. And the Lord said unto Moses, Wherefore criest thou unto me? Speak unto the children of Israel, that they go forward.
(King James Version, Exodus 14:13-15)

Know Jesus

We think of Christianity as a set of rules and regulations. Do this. Don't do that. Being a Christian is much simpler. It's having a relationship with God through Jesus Christ his Son. It's pursuing that love relationship with Him. It is giving your heart and life to another like in marriage. Then you want to please God. You want to talk to Him. You want to be with Him, and He wants to be with you. You are in this together. Being in a relationship with Jesus has totally changed my life!

> We know how much God loves us because we have felt his love and because we believe him when he tells us that he loves us dearly. God is love, and anyone who lives in love is living with God and God is living in him.
>
> (*The Living Bible,* 1 John 4:16)

Trust God

God knows more than I do. He sees the big picture, so He knows that things will work out when I don't. That's why I have to trust Him and not worry or stress when my child is sick, my husband gets laid off, we're low on money, lacking groceries, when my car won't start, or when my load seems heavy.

Even when things look bleak, I can still trust my God. I can trust that He will provide. I can trust and pray for God to intervene. Some things are difficult, but with God, we can walk through it and come out stronger.

> But my God shall supply all your need according to his riches in glory by Christ Jesus.
>
> (*King James Version*, Philippians 4:19)

Fiery Furnace

Do you feel like you are in the middle of a fiery furnace? Do you feel that everything has heated up around you? Do you feel uncomfortable and unsure? Do you feel all alone? Do you wonder where God is? Look, I see Him right there with you!

Just like the three Hebrew boys in Daniel 3, Jesus is right there with you in the midst of the fire! He will deliver you out of this struggle. You are going to come out stronger than before, with more faith and more confidence in God.

> Did not we cast three men bound into the midst of the fire? They answered and said unto the king, True, O king.
>
> He answered and said, Lo, I see four men loose, walking in the midst of the fire, and they have no hurt; and the form of the fourth is like the Son of God.
>
> *(King James Version,* Daniel 3:24-25)

You Can Do This!

Have you ever been to a Little League baseball game for a child that is just learning to play? It's exciting! The parents are so encouraging to the little ones. The fans, coaches, and teammates support the player. There's yelling, clapping, and encouraging. Even if he strikes out, he receives encouragement. They say, "You'll do better next time. At least you were swinging the bat." Everyone gets high fives and pats on the back!

Guess who is in the stands at the baseball game of your life? Your Heavenly Father. He is cheering for you. He is your biggest supporter. He is saying to you, "Stay in the game. Don't get out of the batter's box. Keep your head up. You can do this.

You can do all things through Christ which strengthens you. You are victorious through me. I will never leave you. You are not alone. My child, I love you with an everlasting love. You can do this!!"

I can do all things through Christ which strengtheneth me.

(King James Version, Philippians 4:13)

Delays

How many times have you been delayed by a roadblock or train? It's stopping you, and there is no going around it. It's a barrier in your way. You don't know how long you will be stopped and if it will make you late. It's inconvenient for sure. It's frustrating! You are stuck. Pretty soon cars are lined up behind you all going nowhere.

In Numbers 13-14, the Israelites were finally going into the Promised Land, but there were giants in the way. The giants were occupying the land of milk and honey. The giants were a roadblock stopping the Israelites. Many of them saw the giants and doubted that they could take the land, except for Caleb and Joshua. They believed that they could take the land.

Is there a giant in your life today? Is there a roadblock in your way? Don't look at the obstacles or troubles, but look to God. He is bigger than any problem or difficulty in your life. We have the wrong outlook. We look at this huge, taunting giant, burden, diagnosis, or difficulty and see it looming over us. We see it invading our lives and trying to set up camp; instead, we should look to God.

Don't look at your problem as a mountain or roadblock. Look with eyes of faith. God is bigger! He is mighty! He is able to take down the giants in your life! He wants you to occupy the land! He will bring victory!

> If the Lord delights in us, then he will bring us into this land, and give it to us; a land which floweth with milk and honey. Only rebel not ye against the Lord, neither fear ye the people of the land; for they are bread for us: their defence is departed from them, and the Lord is with us: fear them not.
>
> *(King James Version,* Numbers 13:8-9)

God is at Work

Never doubt that God is at work even if you can't see the outcome yet. Just look at the different people in the Bible. Look at Esther. The whole Jewish people were going to be destroyed because of an evil plot, but God intervened. Esther became queen just for that reason. A young girl saved a nation.

Look at David. A nine-foot giant was standing before the Israelites. No one else would fight Goliath until David came to bring lunch to his brothers. God intervened. A young man that loved the Lord saved an army.

Never doubt that God is at work. He is behind the scenes even if you don't see it yet. Even if it turns out differently than you expected, God is still at work. Trust him. Have faith and believe.

"For I know the plans that I have for you," declares the Lord, "plans to prosper you and not to harm you, plans to give you hope and a future."

(*New International Version*, Jeremiah 29:11)

Who is with you?

Who was in the lion's den with Daniel?
Who was in the fiery furnace with the three
Hebrew boys?
Who was in the boat with the disciples when the
storm came?
Who was with David when he stood before
Goliath?

Who is with you when you go through the storm,
when you're up against a giant, or when you're in
a fiery furnace? Who is with you? Jesus is with
you! With Jesus you have hope, peace, strength,
courage, answers, wisdom, healing, favor, and
direction. Look up! Get your eyes off the problem
and see Jesus!

> When you pass through the waters, I will be
> with you; and when you pass through the
> rivers, they will not sweep over you. When
> you walk through the fire, you will not be
> burned; the flames will not set you ablaze.
> For I am the Lord your God, the Holy One of
> Israel, your Savior.
>
> (*New International Version,* Isaiah 43:2-3a)

God's Strength

I can do all things through Christ which strengthens me, even hump day! Whether it's cold or hot, or cloudy or sunny, I can do this. This is another day of life. Another day with Jesus is sweeter than the day before.

This is the day that the Lord has made I will rejoice and be glad in it! If your day is dreary and cold, walk with Jesus. He will bring you sunshine today!

This is the day which the Lord hath made; we will rejoice and be glad in it.

(*King James Version*, Psalm 118:24)

Victory in Jesus

Declare this out loud:

My victory is in Jesus! In the name of Jesus, I have the victory. I will walk in victory this year, this week, today. I will have victory in my life, my health, my finances, my marriage, my family, my job, and my church.

He is my victory! There is power in the name of Jesus. I am going forth in victory because of Him. I can do nothing without Him but I can do all things with Him! I am victorious! I have the strength, the power, the wisdom, and the grace of the Holy Spirit in me. There's victory in Jesus!

But thanks be to God! He gives us the victory through our Lord Jesus Christ.

(*New International Version*, 1 Corinthians 15:57)

Go Forward in Joy

Usually, I get a word or phrase to live by for the year! One year it was "Be Still." Another year it was "Just Do It!" This year it is, "Go forward in JOY"-Jesus, others, and yourself (myself) and the joy of knowing God.

Let go of your past mistakes, regrets, and things not finished. Go forward with God and let Him lead the way. When you follow Him, then you will have joy!

> For ye shall go out with joy, and be led forth with peace: the mountains and the hills shall break forth before you into singing, and all the trees of the field shall clap their hands.
>
> (*King James Version*, Isaiah 55:12)

Rest

This is one of my favorite verses. I read over and over again and pray it. Then I meditate on what it means to me.

To rest means to trust in God. To be at peace and to know His peace even in a difficult situation, that is resting. When God is your rock that means He is steadfast and faithful. He is my fortress-strong, dependable, and immovable. My faith and confidence in God will not be shaken. No matter what comes my way I am trusting Him so I will not be moved by what I see or feel.

I am standing on rock solid faith in my God. I will not look to the right or left. I will not be distracted by fear or worry. I focus on Him and meditate on His word. I can trust God because I know His character, His faithfulness, and His Word.

After saying it, praying it, and meditating on this verse then I can confidently say, "My soul finds rest in God!"

> Truly my soul finds rest in God; my salvation comes from him. Truly he is my rock and my salvation; he is my fortress, I will never be shaken.
>
> (*New International Version*, Psalm 62:1-2)

God Bless You

I try to say God bless you when someone sneezes.
I write it on birthday and get well cards. When I
say God bless you, I mean so many things. It is
like I am saying a prayer for you.

I am asking God to bless you with His presence
and presents of salvation, love, peace, safety,
health, finances, mercy, grace, wholeness, and
such. May you know Jesus as your Savior and
Lord. May you know Him more and more fully.
May your love for Him deepen and may you know
His love for you.

May you love Him with all your heart, soul, mind,
and strength. May you know and understand His
Word. May you hear His voice and follow after
Him. May you make right, godly choices. May God
show up in your life in a great way. Of course, I
pray this for myself and my family, too.

I am praying for God to bless all that read this
book. I pray that God will bless you
abundantly. And I am thanking God that I am
truly blessed!!

The Lord bless you and keep you; the Lord make
his face shine on you and be gracious to you; the
Lord turn his face toward you and give you
peace.

(*New International Version*, Numbers 6:24-26)

Follow Him

My sheep-I am His sheep; Jesus is my Shepherd. The Shepherd knows best. He will lead and guide us into all safety. He will lead us to provision and see to our needs.

Hear-I will and can hear the voice of my master. Reading His Word and praying will put me in a place to hear clearly. Slowing down and taking time to hear will allow Him to speak. I have ears to hear.

Know-He has a relationship with us. He knew us before we were born. He knows us and loved us. He is our Father.

Follow-Because we know Him, we will follow Him. By following the Good Shepherd, I am doing His will. I can trust my Shepherd. Where He leads, I will follow.

> My sheep hear my voice, and I know them, and they follow me.
>
> (*King James Version*, John 10:27)

Love God

When asked what was the greatest commandment, Jesus answered with Mark 12:30-31. Since it is so important, I pray it often for myself and others. What I love about it that when we love God that much with all our heart, soul, mind, and strength, then we will love others. It is just natural effect from loving God that you love others, too.

Let's pray these verses today for our self and our family, friends, neighbors, and church.

Love the Lord your God with all your heart and with all your soul and with all your mind and with all your strength. The second is this: 'Love your neighbor as yourself.' There is no commandment greater than these."

(*New International Version*, Mark 12:30-31)

Be at Peace

Do not be anxious. Do not go there. Stop the thoughts playing over and over again in your mind. Stop anxiety, doubt, and worry. Don't keep it. Pass it to God like a hot potato that you can't handle. Get it out of your hands. Let go of it. Don't be anxious, be at peace. Hand it off to God in prayer with thanksgiving. God can handle this, let Him!

Prayer:
I speak peace in your situation and to you. I pray for peace like a river to wash over your soul, your mind, your heart, and your emotions. I pray for God's peace that passes all understanding to rule and reign over your emotions.

May God's peace ease the anxiety and fear and calms you. Even in the midst of the battle, may God surround you with peace and comfort. Thank you, God, that You hear our prayers. I pray in Jesus' mighty and precious name. Amen.

Do not be anxious about anything, but in every situation, by prayer and petition, with thanksgiving, present your requests to God.

(*New International Version*, Philippians 4:6)

Get out of the Tomb

The stone being rolled away from Jesus' tomb in Mark 16 reminds me that God prepares the way for us. He rolls stones out of the way so you can be released from what's hindering you. He opens the door to freedom.

The stone was rolled away so Lazarus could come out even though he was dead, he walked out of the tomb alive. Jesus makes that which is dead come to life. He rolls the stone away from our path so that we can go forward. He is calling our name to come forth.

When we accept Jesus in our life, He rolls away our sin, forgives us, and takes the burden from us so we can walk in freedom.

What is in your way? What needs to be removed from your path so that you are free? I pray that the stone that is in your way is moved because Jesus is calling you to come forth!!

> Now the Lord is the Spirit, and where the Spirit of the Lord is, there is freedom.
>
> (*New International Version*, 2 Corinthians 3:17)

Slow and Steady

They say slow and steady wins the race. In my early fifties, I started walking and jogging with some friends. After about six months, we started entering 5K races (3.1 miles) but it was hard especially at the beginning. I had to push myself to finish the race.

Several times I wanted to stop. When it got hard we would slow down or walk a little then start jogging again. I really wasn't worried about winning because to me finishing was winning! Just getting started was winning.

We often say this Christian life is like a race. Thankfully we aren't competing against others. Our goal is to see Jesus, but along the way, we are a work in progress. God will continue that work in us until it's complete, totally complete. He will not stop. He won't give up. If we are determined to continue with God, He will do the work in us.

It may seem difficult at times, but God's grace is sufficient. He is molding and shaping us into the image of His Son. He is working on us! Slow and steady will win this race because God is on our side!

...being confident of this, that he who began a good work in you will carry it on to completion until the day of Christ Jesus.

(*New International Version*, Philippians 1:6)

126

Draw Close to God

They say absence makes the heart grow fonder. Don't believe it. When I slack on a relationship, it feels distant. It's the same with God. We need to keep working on our relationship. God is still with you but you moved away.

What do counselors say to do when you want to fix your relationship? What brings people closer? Being together, doing things together, and communicating-talking and listening. The same is true with God.

If your relationship with God seems lacking. If you need to work on it, then spend time with Him-pray, read His Word, communicate, praise Him, and listen to Him. Be with Him. That will strengthen your relationship. Being together makes the heart grow fonder.

> Draw nigh to God, and
> he will draw nigh to you.
>
> (*King James Version*, Psalm 4:8)

Follow the Leader!

Be at peace.
You may not see the big picture or the outcome,
but God is leading the way.
He is illuminating your every step.
Walk in peace.
Follow the leader!
Keep your eyes on Jesus!

> My whole being follows hard after You and clings closely to You; Your right hand upholds me.
>
> (*Amplified Bible, Classic Edition*, Psalm 63:8)

Victory in Jesus

In high school I went to all the football and basketball games, I even rode the pep bus to away games. I remember most of the cheers. Often a cheer will pop into my mind when I say or hear a certain word like "Let's Go" or "Victory."

Today's cheer is Victory! We are winners. No matter what the enemy or others say, "We win!" And you will win this battle. Stand strong. Stand on solid ground! Victory is yours!

"V-I-C-T (clap, clap, clap)

O-R-Y (clap, clap, clap).

Victory, victory that's our cry!"

> With God we will gain the victory, and he will trample down our enemies.
>
> Psalm 60:12 NIV

Praying for Others

Someone just needs to hear this today. God cares!
I care. I am praying for those that read my books.
I pray that you will know God more and that He
will meet your needs.

There are many times that I would like to help
others, but I am not sure what to do. So, I pray.
Prayer is such a support and it also lets others
know that you care.

I am reminded of the verse-give and it shall be
given unto you. We all have had those times when
others reached out, helped, or prayed for us. It's
time to give back to those in need. Let's make this
a day of prayer.

Give, and it will be given to you. A good
measure, pressed down, shaken together
and running over, will be poured into your
lap. For with the measure you use, it will
be measured to you.

(*New International Version*, Luke 6:38)

Trust Jesus

When I read about Jesus asleep on the boat and how the disciples were afraid because of a storm, I put myself in their place. Would I be at peace in the middle of a storm? I think I would be saying the logical thing, why are we in a boat when there's a storm? We need to get to the shore right now.

I probably would have just run over to Jesus and huddle near Him like a child that wants to sleep with you when they are afraid. Or I might have just stood there staring at him wishing for Him to wake up like a little child that stands in the bedroom looking at you in the dark. You don't see them but you recognize someone staring at you so you are startled awake.

When I am in a storm or difficulty, I am usually the one crying out in fear for God to help me, but I am slowly learning to trust Jesus. He is with me, and He is not sleeping. God help us to trust You like Jesus did!

> Then he got up and rebuked the winds and the waves, and it was completely calm. The men were amazed and asked,
> "What kind of man is this? Even the winds and the waves obey him!"
> (*New International Version*, Matthew 8:27)

Salvation

If you've never asked Jesus in your heart to reign in your life, it is a simple.

First, you must believe that Jesus came to earth to die on a cross for our sins, not his. He was an innocent man, the Son of God. He had no sin but we are sinners. Then you must believe that Jesus not only died on the cross for sinners, but he rose again after three days. Next, you may pray to God to forgive your sin and ask Jesus in your heart. It's that simple. It would be great to tell others about this.

Salvation Prayer:

God, I believe that Jesus is your Son and that He died on a cross for my sins but He came back alive in three days. I ask You to forgive me for my sin. I am sorry.

Jesus, come into my heart and life. I want to know you more. Help me to understand salvation. I want to love you. Show me how. Lead and guide my life. Help me to live for you. Thank you for your love for me. Thank you for my salvation. I pray in Jesus' name. Amen.

Salvation Scriptures

For all have sinned, and come short of the glory of God. Romans 3:23 KJV

But God commendeth his love toward us, in that, while we were yet sinners, Christ died for us. Romans 5:8 KJV

For as by one man's disobedience many were made sinners, so by the obedience of one shall many be made righteous.

Moreover the law entered, that the offence might abound. But where sin abounded, grace did much more abound: That as sin hath reigned unto death, even so might grace reign through righteousness unto eternal life by Jesus Christ our Lord. Romans 5:19-21 KJV

For God so loved the world, that he gave his only begotten Son, that whosoever believeth in him should not perish, but have everlasting life. For God sent not his Son into the world to condemn the world; but that the world through him might be saved. John 3:16-17 KJV

Neither is there salvation in any other: for there is none other name under heaven given among men, whereby we must be saved. Acts 4:12 KJV

That if thou shalt confess with thy mouth the Lord Jesus, and shalt believe in thine heart that God hath raised him from the dead, thou shalt be saved. For with the heart man believeth unto righteousness; and with the mouth confession is made unto salvation. Romans 10:9-10 KJV

For whosoever shall call upon the name of the Lord shall be saved. Romans 10:13 KJV

Therefore if any man be in Christ, he is a new creature: old things are passed away; behold, all things are become new. 2 Corinthians 5:17 KJV

For by grace are ye saved through faith; and that not of yourselves: it is the gift of God: Not of works, lest any man should boast. Ephesians 2:8-9 KJV

About the author:

Tammy Dozier Trusty is a retired teacher, wife, mother of two, and grandmother of six. She loves spending time with family, friends, and quiet times with God. She loves the simple pleasures in life like road trips, God's creation, reading a good book and the good book, Bible study, being with her husband, and watching her children and now grandchildren's activities.

She has spent her life dedicated to loving and serving God through her teaching, writing, and praying. She's served as the Prayer Director at her church for many years.

Following God's heart is her main priority. She prays that each reader is inspired, encouraged, dares to dream and one's faith increases as they read this book!

All her books are available on Amazon.